Contents

Getting Started

Digital cameras are cameras that take pictures without film. The camera records the photograph as a computer file on a little card, disc or memory stick.

How they work

Cameras break every photograph into tiny segments called pixels. When put together like a giant puzzle, they create a whole photograph. The more pixels in your photograph, the higher the resolution. Higher resolution photographs have more detail. Low resolution, photographs might look nice on your computer monitor, but if you try to print them too big the quality will be very poor.

Pixels are like tiny puzzle pieces(left), each with a little bit of the picture on it. When combined in the proper order, they create a whole picture (below).

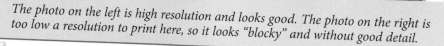

The photo on the left is high resolution and looks good. The photo on the right is too low a resolution to print here, so it looks "blocky" and without good detail.

Getting your photographs

Once you've taken a photograph, you can transfer it to your computer. Attach your camera with cord that goes into the computer. Then save the images onto the computer – that way you'll have quick access to them. Turning your pictures into photographs you can hold is easy if you have a home printer. If not, you can send the images to a printer through an online website or take the memory card into a shop to have them printed.

After you've finished shooting, you can remove the memory card from your camera and put it in a card port or a card reader.

Some companies are now creating cameras that connect directly to the Internet using Wi-Fi! This means that it's easy to upload photos to social media websites, or send an image quickly in an email.

The advantage of digital

There are many reasons to use digital cameras rather than cameras that use film. You can use software to improve your photograph, or turn them into complete artistic creations. Programs like Adobe® Photoshop® Elements, iPhoto and Microsoft Photo Gallery let you do all sorts of fun and creative things to your pictures.

Choosing a camera

When picking a digital camera, choosing one with higher the megapixels will enable you to make big prints from your pictures. Professional higher resolution cameras (megapixel numbers over 16) can be a lot more expensive.

Look for a lens with a good zoom range, such as 5X or 15X. A nice big monitor is great too so you can check your pictures or share them with friends. Check the controls too. They should be easy to access and simple to understand.

Lastly, hold the camera in your hand. Does it feel good? Is it easy to hold without covering the lens or flash?

Select a camera that is right for you. Look for a model with the right number of megapixels, a good zoom and, most importantly, one that you feel comfortable using.

The Basics

Although they look complicated, cameras are easy to use. To take a picture, the camera needs to let light into the lens to record on the image sensor. This happens when you push the shutter button. The quality of picture you then get depends on how you use the camera and its many features.

flash
zoom lens

Stay sharp

Digital cameras have automatic (or auto) focus. That means that if your subject and your camera are still the whole time the shutter is open, the picture will be sharp (in focus). But if the subject moves, or the camera shakes, it will be blurry (out of focus).

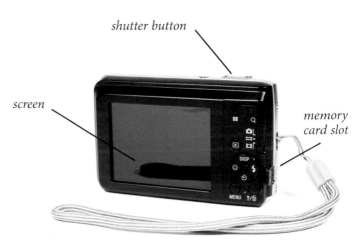
shutter button
screen
memory card slot

This picture of Samson is sharp.

This picture is blurred because it is out of focus.

KEY SKILLS

If you find you are producing blurry pictures, hold your camera very steady. If your subject is a few metres or less away, turn on the flash. And if your camera has "ISO" controls, change it to the highest number in dim light. Remember to switch it back to Auto ISO when the lighting gets brighter!

In the first two images, the background is in the centre (see yellow circle) so it is in focus. In the second two images, Focus Lock was used on the girl and and the photograph was retaken. Now the kids are in focus.

KEY SKILLS

Some cameras try and focus on whatever is in the middle of the picture. But often, the best pictures have an off-centred subject! If you find your subject is blurry but the background looks great, you need to use Focus Lock. To achieve this:

- Centre the camera on the subject,
- Push the shutter button halfway down to lock the focus,
- Then (without lifting your finger) reposition the camera so the picture is how you want it,
- Push the shutter the remaining way to click the picture.

Close-ups

You can sometimes get out of focus pictures if you are too close to your subject. Does your camera have a "close-up" or "macro" mode? This may be indicated by a symbol of a flower. If you are closer than a metre or so from your subject, you may need to switch to this mode.

Use the screen!

It's fun to review your pictures on the monitor after you shoot them. It's also helpful to make sure you got the shot, and to see if you can make improvements. Check focus, expressions and composition (pages 10-11).

Don't forget to zoom

A good technique in photography is to fill the picture up with as much of the subject as you can. If your camera has a zoom, use the Tele or T setting to make your subject bigger in the final picture.

DID YOU KNOW?

Printer inks and papers cost a LOT of money. So don't print something, unless you're sure you really want a copy. Talk with your parents and set a "printing supplies allowance" so nobody is surprised when the ink or paper runs out.

All About Light

Bright sunlight makes your pictures feel very bold. However it can cast deep dark shadows. If these shadows are behind the subject (like in the kitten photograph) this is good, but if they are on your friend's face they can be bad because it might hide their features.

Fight the light

It's usually best to have the people you are photographing facing the sun. This will mean the sun is at your back. If your subject is wearing a hat with a brim, or you see big shadows on their face, turn on your camera's flash unit. Controls called Force Flash or Fill Flash will do a good job.

Overcast days are great for portraits, because there are only soft-edged shadows that aren't very dark. This usually means you'll get a more flattering picture.

DID YOU KNOW?

Fluorescent lighting (those long tubes found in many classrooms) has a greenish colour. You can't really see it with your eyes, but the camera might see it. Sunlight looks normal to the camera, but regular household lamp light bulbs look yellowish, and shadows are bluish. Some cameras can modify these colours so they look "correct", but sometimes you'll see the colour cast in the pictures.

Light from behind

If the light is behind your subject, such as a sunset in the distance, you will get a silhouette. This means that the backlit subject (a person, horse, or whatever) will look black, without any detail. This isn't bad – in fact it can make for some very pretty pictures.

This gecko is having a look at us over the top of a big leaf. He thinks he's hidden – and he would be if the sun wasn't hitting the back of the leaf. When an object is backlit, it will either block the light (opaque) or allow the light to shine through (transparent). His body blocks the sunlight, so it is the only part of the leaf that is dark. The rest of the leaf glows with the light.

KEY SKILL

When the light is dim, but pretty, turn your flash off (usually indicated by a symbol of a lightning bolt with the circle-slash over it). Candlelight is a great example of dim but pretty light. Any time you turn the flash off, be sure to hold the camera steady or the picture will be blurred. Try bracing it against a wall, or steadying it on a table. Then tell your model to stand very, very still!

DID YOU KNOW?

Painters from hundreds of years ago (long before photography was invented) used to put their subjects next to a north-facing window, because the light was soft and pretty, just like in this photograph. In painting and photography, *soft light* means your can barely see any shadows. This tends to make people look really good.

Composition

Making your pictures prettier is called improving the composition. Certain elements make up the composition, the most important being the main subject. The background and foreground is also a part of the composition, as are things that are put in the picture area either on purpose or by accident.

A tulip garden

Choosing your options

Where and how all these elements (the main subject, other objects and the foreground and background) appear in your photograph will have a big effect on the success of the picture. If your schoolteacher said, "Photograph a pink tulip" most people would do a quick snapshot of a garden with tulips. But you can be much more creative than that. Below are just a few options. Can you think of more?

Fill the space

One of the easiest ways to improve a picture is to fill the picture with nothing but subject. To do this, zoom in to Tele (T) or step closer to your subject. Notice how in the first photo, your friends are fairly small in the picture. But by stepping closer and zooming in, they are now a much bigger (and more important) part of the picture.

A single tulip

Tulip petals!

A girl & tulips

Backlit tulips

A tulip bunch

Wide

Tele

GETTING IT RIGHT !

Pay attention to the background when you are taking a photograph. Otherwise, you might be surprised to see things "growing" out of your subject's head. A tree can look like antlers, and this Ferris wheel looks like a hat or halo. Check the background for surprises like this!

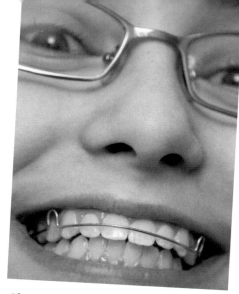

If your camera has a Close-Up mode, you can really fill the frame!

Off the centre

The best compositions do not have your subject in the dead centre of the picture! Try to put more important parts of the picture (like the flip-flops and sunglasses shown right) to the sides of the picture. If you draw an imaginary grid over the picture and place the important parts of the picture along the lines. When shooting an off-centre subject, you should use Focus Lock (see page 7). Eyes are important parts of a portrait, so put them off-centre.

Bad

Good – room to move into

Leaving space

Another important way to put your subject off centre is to leave "space" in front of where a person is looking or about to move into. Compare these shots of the swimming girl. In the best version, the boy has "extra" water in front of him, and this makes the best composition.

Lines

Lines that appear in your photographs are very important elements in your composition. Curving lines tend to make a picture seem lively (left). Straight and diagonal lines, like the cables on a bridge, can make a bold picture (right).

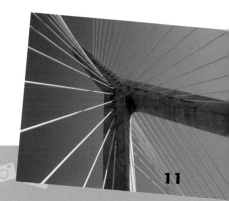

11

Pe. fect Po. t. a it:

One of the best reasons to use your camera is to take portraits of your friends and family. Not only are they fun to have now, but weeks, months and even years from now it will be great to see them in your album.

Above: Shooting with the lens at Wide and moving in close causes distortions.

Below: Shooting with the lens at Tele and moving far away is more flattering.

Use your zoom

The best way to take a serious portrait is to step way back from the person you are shooting, and zoom the lens all the way to the Tele (T) setting. On some cameras, the zoom setting will be marked with a symbol of a single tree (instead of a "T" or Tele), and a lot of little trees (instead of a "W" or Wide). If your camera does not have a zoom lens, you can change the size of the person in your picture by stepping closer or further away.

Filling a picture

Use your zoom if your camera has it, and make the person you are photographing fill the entire picture. This girl was surrounded with boring grass, so her friend zoomed the camera to Tele (T) until no grass was showing. The result is an amazing portrait.

KEY SKILLS

One of the bad things about being the photographer is that you're not in any of the pictures unless you do a self-portrait. You can balance your camera on a fence post or table, or use a small tripod, to take self-portraits. Then use the self-timer control. This will give you about 10 seconds to "run into" the scene before the camera shoots the picture.

Choosing details

Who says you have to show the whole face? You can zoom in really close on your subject for an unusual (but really great) effect. You can also do this later on the computer by using software to "crop" a picture. Cropping means you just "cut off" some of the outside of the picture to make it look better.

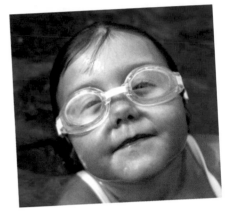

Wide zoom

Using wide-zoom provides includes the surroundings in the photograph. While Tele is used more for portraits, the wide zoom is great for landscape photographs.

An example of using the wide zoom setting is when you want to show more than just the people. This picture (right) is a portrait of the family, but it tells us about their home as well.

Posing Possibilities

Plain old portraits are fine, but don't forget to have some fun! There are lots of ways to make portraits more fun.

Photographing friends

The first shot of four friends (top right) was the first quick shot. But then she had everyone lie down with their hands on their chins and she shot from a lying down position. But for the third shot, the photographer put everyone on their backs, with their heads together and stood over them to take the picture.

Build a pyramid

Human pyramids make great photos, too. Have the biggest kids on the bottom, and the smallest on top. Don't try it with more than 3 people unless there are adults around who can make sure nobody gets hurt falling.

GETTING IT RIGHT

Plunging into the pool is a pretty cool pose too! But make sure you stand far enough back to keep the camera dry. If it gets wet it could stop working. Keep a Ziplock type of bag around and put the camera in it after you shoot. This will keep it safe from splashes when you're not using it.

Stacking up

Are your sisters and brothers all different ages and sizes? Have fun "stacking" them in size order. Not only does it look good, but also in a year or two it will be fun to see how much everyone has grown.

If your friends are good at gymnastics, take advantage of their skills. Ask them to hold the pose while you take the shot. Then swap places and have them photograph you. Most of all, have fun!

As long as it's safe and you have permission from your parents, there are few limits on creative posing. Don't forget to check out the Funny Photos section (pages 20-21) and Try This section (pages 26-29) for more posing ideas.

TOP TIP

It can add a nice feeling of unity to a picture to have everyone dress the same. These sisters are 12 years apart in age, but their clothing makes them seem linked. And you'll look like a team if you all wear the same coloured shirts.

At an Angle

Usually it is best to shoot portraits of people and pets from their eye level. This is a pretty good rule. But rules are made to be broken, and sometimes crazy angles yield interesting results.

Shoot from below

Looking up at one of your friends makes them look really tall. You can get this kind of shot by sitting or lying on the ground and having them stand over you. This is probably what you look like to your baby brother or dog!

This cat is about five metres high in the tree. By zooming the lens to Wide and pointing the camera straight up at her, she looks like she's a whole lot higher!

KEY SKILLS

You usually want to hold your camera as straight as possible so the picture looks straight. But every once in a while, try turning your camera slightly. Sometimes taking a crooked shot on purpose can give and interesting look to the picture. A little tilt can create diagonal lines, and this can sometimes make a plain old photo look livelier.

Using humour

It is pretty funny to look up at a reindeer at a zoo – and he probably thinks you look pretty funny sitting on the ground to take a shot like this!

Shoot from above

Try finding a high spot to look down from, like a tall porch or the climbing frame at a playground. If your friends are on the ground, and you're high up, it will look like a bird's-eye view. Even standing over a sitting person can give an interesting angle too.

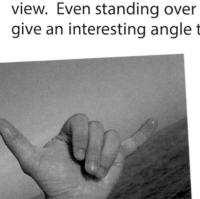

At an angle

In photo-editing software like Adobe® Photoshop® Elements or PaintShop Pro®, you can rotate a picture to straighten it or make it a little off kilter. This "Hang Loose" Hawaiian hand signal (left) looks really interesting when the ocean is tilted. Try it and see.

KEY SKILLS

Here's a really fun technique, but you'll need the help of an adult for safety. Lie on the ground next to a picnic table and point the camera up. Then have your baby sister stand on the table and pretend to step off the table (but of course, an adult will be holding her just out of view of the camera, so she doesn't fall and hurt both of you!). The result will look like she's a giant and you're an ant.

Using Colour

Colour is everywhere! Even "pure" white subjects like snow have colour and tone. "White" can be warm/yellowish or cold/bluish. Understanding colour can turn a good photograph into a great picture.

The colour blue is associated with the words cold and winter, so it gives the picture an even more wintry feel.

Red is associated with anger, so the background colour enhances this girl's funny "mean" face. It also makes the picture look almost like a cartoon!

Colours and moods

People associate certain colours with certain moods or words, so colour can have a big impact on your picture. For example, blue is usually cool and refreshing. Red is hot and powerful, and sometimes associated with danger. Yellow is bright and cheery. Metallic chrome is cold and steely.

Red and green are considered the colours of Christmas, so putting a red cap on this snowman reinforce the holiday feeling.

Colour combinations

Certain colours used together have a significance of their own, especially if they represent the colour of a national flag. That's why the uniform colours on most World Cup teams match that nation's flag colours. Other symbolic colour associations include green and red for Christmas.

TOP TIP

Check your cupboards for some fun and colourful accessories, like a blue scarf, a red bandana, or a colourful old sun hat. How can you use them in photographs of your friends to add to the picture?

Grabbing attention

Colour that is unrelated to the subject can be very distracting, but if the colour "accents" the subject by attracting our attention, it can be good. For example, the red colour of this girl's helmet (left) pulls our attention to her face. And the pink of the flowers in the background of the portrait shot below are similar to the colours in the girl's shirt, and the pink of her lips. This creates a very pleasing picture.

Yellow and blue are opposite or conflicting colours, so this yellow duck stands out boldly from the blue pool.

Working with colour

Different colours can be harmonious (pleasing next to each other) or conflicting (fight with each other). This yellow duck in a blue pool stands out a lot more than a red or green toy would, because yellow and blue are conflicting colours – they are "opposites" in the world of colour.

The red mouth of the duck matches the background for a picture that has nice visual harmony.

This boy pulled his t-shirt halfway on for a funny portrait. But the red colour makes a nice frame around his face.

Funny Photos

What makes a photograph funny? A lot of
different things. It can be a funny situation or a
funny face. You can make a pun or tell a joke.
You can cause something big to look small, and
something small to look big. Or you can use
your camera controls to make something
look distorted and silly.

Making people laugh

What makes you laugh? Some situations are just
funny. Does your baby brother make a mess at
dinnertime? Time to get your camera! Does your cat
climb into the wash basin? Time to get your camera.
Funny situations like these make great photos. If you
carry your camera in your pocket or knapsack, you'll be
ready for anything.

If you can tell a joke or make a pun in your picture, that's
funny. Look at the picture on the right. Not only is this a
funny picture, but it is a funny pun. This person is wearing
glasses instead of *glasses*. Check around the kitchen.
Glasses with the clearest bottom will work best. Add a
funny expression and the picture gets even more amusing.

Are they glasses or glasses?

DID YOU KNOW?

Over a hundred years ago, when photography
was fairly new, people loved to buy or pose for funny
picture postcards, which they mailed to their friends.
There was no such thing as a phone, the Internet,
aeroplanes or even cars, so the mail was the only way to
keep in touch with distant friends and relatives.

20

Funny faces

You can't go wrong with funny faces! Cross-eyed friends, fish-mouth talking, blown-up cheeks and more. Add silly props like glasses or hats to heighten the effect. Zoom in close for funny distortions or tilt the camera for an unbalanced feeling. Don't forget about adults – everyone expects kids to be silly, but when your parents make strange faces it can be *really* funny!

TOP TIP

Try using the camera on your mobile to take fun photos! Once you take a photo of your friend, pet or parent, you can easily send the photo to a friend in a text message.

Animals make funny faces too!

Words in a photograph can be funny too, like this "No Parking" sign that was changed.

Bad dog! Doesn't he know how to read the sign?

This photo is funny because it looks like the cat is winning the game of hide-and-seek...

TOP TIP

Don't forget to go against gravity! If you photograph a friend hanging upside-down from a climbing frame or tree limb, their hair will fall down. Rotate the photo before you print it (turn it upside-down), and it will look like their hair is sticking straight up! This works best for kids with long hair.

Sports & Action

Pictures of sports and other action are some of the hardest to take. Things move fast, and you need to be ready to catch the moment. If you have an Action or Sports mode on your camera (usually indicated by a picture of a running man), use it! And play with your zoom lens to make the action bigger in the viewfinder or on the camera's monitor.

Beat the blur

Ever wonder why some of your action pictures are blurry? Here's why. Let's imagine your friend is dribbling a football while the camera is taking the picture. The imaging sensor in the camera might "see" him in several different places, and a little bit of him will record in each place, so he will look blurry in the photo. In bright light, this won't happen as often, because the camera needs to keep the shutter open for only a short amount of time (see page 6). But on dark days or when shooting indoors, the camera needs to leave the shutter open longer to make a picture, and your friend might be able to run a step or two during that time, so he will look very blurred in the picture. The faster he is running, the more he will blur!

Faster moving things blur more than slower moving things. Here the ball is rolling (and spinning) faster than the boy is running, so it is blurred more!

The Panning Technique

Without Panning

You'll get less blurry action pictures if you learn the panning technique. This means, you should follow your subject in the viewfinder or monitor *before*, *during* and *after* you take the picture. The result will be much sharper pictures. And even if they're blurry, they may still look better.

With Panning

Sports are more than just action! Look for pictures that tell a story about the game, like this team cheer picture.

Are you getting a long delay between when you push the shutter button and when the camera takes the picture? If so, it is probably because your camera is having trouble focusing on the fast-moving action. Try using Focus Lock (see page 7) when the action is predictable. For example, prefocus on the ball before a penalty or corner kick, and wait. Then push the shutter button all the way down when the player goes to kick.

You start panning by planting your feet on the ground, about 35cm apart. Then twist at the waist. As the action goes by, follow it by turning at the waist. Don't move your feet! And try to have all the movement come from your waist.

Use your zoom lens to get closer to the action, or crop the picture later when it is on your computer. You can even simplify the picture in the computer by removing other people with software.

Cropping an image

Sometimes it's hard to get up close to the action. And even after you zoom your camera all the way to Tele (T), the people still look small. Take the picture anyway. Later, when it is on the computer, you can use software to crop it.

Cropping is easy. It just means you "cut" off all the extra stuff — like taking a pair of scissors and cutting the centre out of a print (only you're doing it on the computer). The only downside to cropping is that you will make the picture a lower resolution (see page 4) because you are throwing away part of it .

Training sessions are a good time to take sports photos. Try standing behind the net.

Panning works, because you are moving the camera at the same speed as the subject. So if the subject stays in the centre of the viewfinder (and in the centre of the digital imaging sensor), it's as if they are standing still in the camera.

Perfect Pets

Photographing your dog, cat, bird or other pet can be hard – but it's also a lot of fun. You can use all the portrait tips on pages 12-13 for pets. Here are a few more to help you.

Ground level

The best and faster way to get great portraits of your pet is to get down to their eye level. With a puppy, this means lying on the ground! If you have a big dog, and it is standing, you'll need to hold the camera at waist level or kneel down.

You can raise up a small animal so you are eye level with them.

Shooting from this kitten's eye level makes this a great photo. He's on a couch, so kneeling will get you to his eye level.

A car is a great place to take a portrait of your dog.

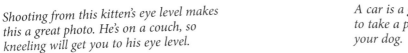

There are two basic ways to take great pet portraits.

If you want the photograph to be really, really *cute* do this:

1 Stand up and move close to your pet
2 Zoom the camera to Wide (W)
3 Point the camera down at your pet
4 Get their attention with food or a noise so they look up, then click

Shooting close and zooming to the Wide (W) will make your dog look goofy and cute.

But if you want a traditional, *beautiful* portrait, do this:

1 Zoom the camera all the way to Tele (T)
2 Step way, way back
3 Squat down to their eye level

Stepping further away and zooming to Tele (T) will make the dog look prettier or more handsome.

Keep them still

If you find your pet won't stay still for long, try and figure out a fun way to make him want to stay! You can put out a pile of food for your guinea pig or hamster. Or have a pocketful of treats to reward a dog or cat for being good.

Another great way to keep your pet still long enough for a photo is to put them into a box or other container. A car can be a container for a dog! A glass can be a container for a gerbil! For tiny pets that are easily frightened, you can have someone hold them in their hand for the picture.

An Easter basket is just the right size for this 3-week-old kitten!

Close-up

Don't look through the viewfinder – just zoom the camera to Wide (W) and stick the camera about half a metre from your dog or cat's face. Then take pictures while you get closer and closer. How close can you get and still have the animal in focus? How close can you get before your cat or dog gets up and moves?

Having a friend or parent hold your pets is an excellent way to photograph them without the risk of them running away or falling off a table.

KEY SKILLS

Practice making funny noises. Squeaking, "meowing" or high pitched noises can sometimes get your pet to look at the camera or put on a great expression.

TOP TIP

You should try and make photography fun for your pet, so have lots of treats on hand. Reward them for good behaviour. If they're being "bad" it probably just means they're confused or bored. If this happens, put down your camera and play with your pet awhile, then try again later.

This puppy poking out of a plastic storage box makes a nice photograph and he can't run away while you are taking it.

Try This!

Sometimes you might find it difficult to come up with ideas for your photographs. The themes below might help get you started.

This lion picture was taken by putting the camera right up against the viewing glass at a zoo. He's not roaring, he's yawning!

Farms and zoos

Farms are great places to take pictures. The animals may come right up to you – in fact you might even have trouble keeping them far enough away to take pictures! Traditional zoos are a little harder. The best shots can be taken when the animals are behind glass rather than bars. You can then put the camera right up against the glass to take pictures.

Fish tanks

Your home fish tank or hamster cage is great for photographs. Turn off your flash, and put your camera right against the glass! If you find your pictures are out of focus, you may need to use the Focus Lock function (see page 7). Turn your flash off if it causes reflections. If you shoot from a few inches away from the glass, try different angles to minimize the reflections.

You can take pictures of your fish by putting the camera right up against the glass.

You can shoot hamsters, lizards and other small animals in their terrarium.

Magnifying glass

Have a family member or one of your friends hold a magnifying glass up to their eye. Ask them to move it closer and further away until it looks best, with a giant eye visible. For the strongest effect, try to have them hold it so it is not twisted away from you. Then take the picture!

Face painting

Whether you're going to a costume party, a school football match, or just messing about, face painting can be fun. It can also be a great photograph. After the painting is done, shoot the picture somewhere in the shade. Flash or bright sunlight might make the paint look greasy or produce weird highlights.

It's a splash

The pool or water sprinkler is the best place to be on a hot sunny day! It's also the best spot for photos. Ask you friends to do crazy stuff, like dump a bucket of water on their head. But watch out! Take some precautions to keep your camera dry. Leave it in a Ziplock type bag until you're ready to shoot. Then pick a shooting angle that is a safe distance from the water or splashing.

Try This!

Sci-fi photos

Build a clay monster (above), or bring some plastic animals out into your garden, and you can create a great science fiction picture. Sand and pebbles can look like a desert. Some rocks can look like an alien planet. And tall grass can seem like a forest!

Check and see if you camera has a Close-up Mode (often indicated by an icon of a flower). This will help you get sharp pictures of little subjects.

Landscapes

If you see a pretty landscape, be sure to use all the composition tips on pages 10-11. Put the skyline in the top third or bottom third of the picture. The best pictures put the horizon (where land or water meets sky) high or low (right) in the picture . If possible, design a landscape picture so there is something in the front, like a person or a flower. Showing someone or something gives the picture a focal point, and helps show the scale of the scene.

Playing Dress Up

Sometimes it's fun to play dress-up, whether it is for a costume party, a school play or dance, or an American-style Halloween celebration. Don't forget your camera! It's a great way to get fantastic pictures of your friends.

Shadow play

Don't forget about shadows! Direct sunlight will cause shadows, and sometimes these shadows are really good to shoot. You don't have to actually show an object to take a picture of it. Look at the photo of the basketball hoop on the right – the picture just shows the shadow. A shadow is also a good design element. The image of the witch (bottom right) looks very scary when you just see the shadow. The shadows on the boy's face (below) also make for an interesting portrait.

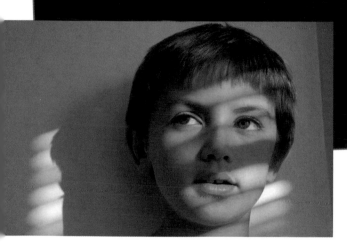

Scanner Photos

If you have a flatbed scanner attached to your computer, it's almost like having a second camera. A scanner just takes pictures of flat (or relatively flat) objects. You can take a scanner picture of your artwork, old ticket stubs, flowers, or even your favorite stuffed animal. Just lay it on the scanner's glass and close the lid. If the object is too "fat" to close the lid, drape a cloth over it. Never put your face on the scanner, or look at the light while it is scanning.

Glossary

AutoFlash
Automated flash mode. It usually fires the flash in low-light situations.

Autofocus
The camera automatically focuses on what it thinks is the main subject.

Composition
A term for how a picture is designed.

Download
To transfer pictures from your camera to computer, or Internet to computer.

Fill Flash
A flash mode that fires the camera's built-in or accessory flash to add some front lighting to the subject.

Focus
The sharpness of an image

Focus Lock
Feature that lets you take off-centred pictures that are properly focused.

ISO
This figure indicates a camera's low-light capability, with a higher number being better. Usually called Equivalent ISO.

Megabyte (MB)
A measurement of file size (1000 bytes).

Megapixel
1,000,000 pixels. Often used to indicate the resolution of a camera.

Optical Zoom
A camera feature that makes your subject look like it is closer.

Panning
Technique that helps you get sharper images, especially of moving subjects.

Pixel
A single picture element that, when combined with others, creates a digital photograph.

Port
A place on your computer, camera or scanner where you can connect it to another device.

Resolution
The number of pixels that make up a digital image. More pixels (higher resolution) means more quality, but also larger file sizes.

Scanner
A machine that turns a print, film or flat artwork into a digital picture.

Tele
A lens setting that makes the subject look closer than it actually is.

Viewfinder
A viewing window that you bring up to your eye to compose pictures.

Zoom
A type of lens that allows you to zoom from a wide view of the scene to a closer look at your subject (Tele).

Web Links

**www.betterphoto.com/
photography-for-kids.asp**
The website of Better Photo.com, a guide for
children learning how to take digital
photographs.

**http://library.thinkquest.org/28146/
home.shtml**
A selection of courses that teach about different
aspects of photography, from how to take great
photographs to the history of photography.

**www.adobe.com/education/digkids/
index.html**
Software company Adobe's guide to digital
photography for children.

**http://kids-myshot.
nationalgeographic.com/**
A website where you can upload your photos, as
well as look at other kids' images.

http://www.shortcourses.com/use/
A website that teaches you everything you may
need or want to know about digital photography.

**http://photography.
nationalgeographic.com/
photography/photo-tips/**
Photography tips from the National
Geographic magazine.

**www.edutainingkids.com/articles/
digitalcamerafunlearning.html**
Site teaching children how to use digital cameras.

**http://www.youthlearn.org/
taxonomy/term/30**
Site aimed at parents giving them help teaching
children how to use digital cameras.

Note to parents and teachers
Every effort has been made by the Publishers
to ensure that the websites in this book are
suitable for children, that they are of the highest
educational value, and that they contain no
inappropriate or offensive material. However,
because of the nature of the Internet, it is
impossible to guarantee that the contents of
these sites will not be altered. We strongly
advise that Internet access is supervised by
a responsible adult.

Index